FRETBOARD ROADMAPS BLUES GUITAR

THE ESSENTIAL GUITAR PATTERNS THAT ALL THE PROS KNOW AND USE

BY FRED SOKOLOW

To access audio visit:
www.halleonard.com/mylibrary

Enter Code
7729-7018-0152-4755

The Recording
Guitar and Vocals—Fred Sokolow
Sound Engineer and Other Instruments—Denis O'Hanlon
Recorded at O'Hanlon Recording and Music Services

ISBN 978-0-634-00114-0

HAL•LEONARD®
7777 W. BLUEMOUND RD. P.O. BOX 13819 MILWAUKEE, WI 53213

Visit Hal Leonard Online at
www.halleonard.com

FRETBOARD ROADMAPS BLUES GUITAR

THE ESSENTIAL GUITAR PATTERNS THAT ALL THE PROS KNOW AND USE

CONTENTS

3   **INTRODUCTION**

4   **HOW TO READ CHORD GRIDS**

4   **HOW TO READ THE FRETBOARD DIAGRAMS**

5   #1   **NOTES ON THE FRETBOARD**
Tips on how to learn them.

6   #2   **THE MAJOR SCALE**
Understanding intervals.

8   #3   **TWO MOVEABLE MAJOR CHORDS**
Barred E and A chords, root notes, blues progressions.

10   #4   **VARIATIONS OF THE TWO MOVEABLE MAJOR CHORDS**
A shortcut to learning hip blues chords.

13   #5   **THE I–IV–V CHORD FAMILY**
Using moveable chords to play 12- and 8-bar blues, and boogie licks.

17   #6   **THE F–D–A ROADMAP**
Using three major chord fragments to follow a chord through its inversions.

20   #7   **FIRST POSITION BLUES BOXES**
Playing blues solos and tunes in the first few frets.

25   #8   **THE FIRST AND SECOND MOVEABLE BLUES BOXES**
Moveable patterns for soloing up the neck.

30   #9   **THE THIRD AND FOURTH MOVEABLE BLUES BOXES**
More moveable patterns for up-the-neck soloing.

34   #10   **MOVEABLE TURNAROUNDS AND BACKUP LICKS**
A moveable lick played on the first and third strings, and more turnarounds.

37   #11   **BOOGIE WOOGIE LICKS: THE MAJOR PENTATONIC SCALE**
Two sliding scales and how to use them for blues riffs.

40   **USING THE PRACTICE TRACKS**

INTRODUCTION

Accomplished blues guitarists can ad lib blues solos and play backup in any key—all over the fretboard. They know several different soloing approaches and can choose the style that fits the tune.

There are moveable patterns on the guitar fretboard that make it easy to do these things. The pros are aware of these "Fretboard Roadmaps," even if they don't read music. If you want to play blues with other players, *this is essential guitar knowledge.*

You need the fretboard roadmaps if…

▶ All your soloing sounds the same and you want some different styles and flavors from which to choose.

▶ Some keys are harder to play in than others.

▶ Your guitar fretboard beyond the 5th fret is mysterious, uncharted territory.

▶ You can't automatically play any blues lick you can think or hum.

▶ You know some blues scales, but don't know how to connect one to another.

▶ You know a lot of "bits and pieces" on the guitar, but you don't have a system that ties it all together.

Read on, and many mysteries will be explained. If you're serious about playing acoustic or electric blues, the pages that follow can shed light and save you a great deal of time.

Good luck,

FRED SOKOLOW

This book is a blues guitarist's extension of Fred Sokolow's *Fretboard Roadmaps* (Hal Leonard Corporation, HL00696514), which includes even more music theory for guitarists, along with musical examples, solos and licks. We urge you to use *Fretboard Roadmaps* as a reference, along with *Fretboard Roadmaps for the Blues Guitarist.*

THE RECORDING AND THE PRACTICE TRACKS

All the licks, riffs and tunes in this book are played on the accompanying audio tracks.

There are also five *practice tracks* on the recording. Each one has a standard blues groove and progression. They are mixed so that the lead guitar is on one side of your stereo and the backup band is on the other.

Each track illustrates the use of certain techniques, such as the first blues box or double-note licks.

You can also tune out the lead guitar track and use the backup tracks to practice playing solos.

HOW TO READ CHORD GRIDS

A *chord grid* is a picture of three or four frets of the guitar's fretboard. The dots show you where to fret (finger) the strings:

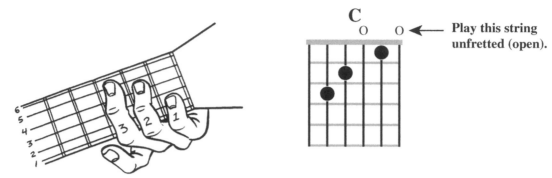

Play this string unfretted (open).

Numbers on a grid indicate the fingering. The number to the right of the grid is a *fret number.*

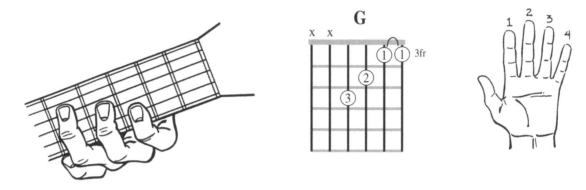

HOW TO READ THE FRETBOARD DIAGRAMS

Each fretboard diagram is a schematic picture of the guitar's fretboard, as it appears when you look down at it while playing.

▶ The 6th, heaviest string is at the bottom; the 1st, lightest string is on top.

▶ Crucial fret numbers such as 5, 7 and 10 are indicated below the 6th string.

▶ *Dots* on the fretboard indicate where you fret the strings (as in chord grids).

▶ *Numbers* on the fretboard indicate which finger to use (1=index finger, 2=middle finger, etc.)

▶ *Letters* on the fretboard are "notes" (A, B♭, C♯, etc.).

▶ *Roman Numerals* (I, IV, etc.) on the fretboard are roots of chords.

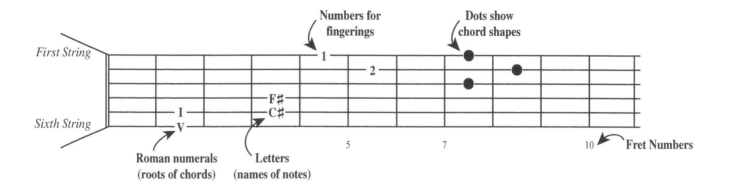

#1 NOTES ON THE FRETBOARD

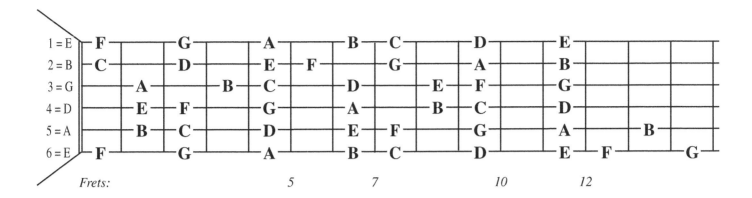

WHY?

▶ Knowing where the notes are (especially the notes on the 6th and 5th strings) will help you find chords up and down the neck. It will help you alter and understand chords (*e.g., How do I flat the seventh in this chord? Why is this chord minor instead of major?*). It's also a first step toward reading music.

WHAT?

▶ *The notes get higher in pitch as you go up the alphabet and up the fretboard.*

▶ *Whole steps and half steps:* A whole step is two frets; a half step is one fret.

▶ *Sharps are one fret higher:* 6th string/3rd fret = G, so 6th string/4th fret = G♯; 6th string/8th fret = C, so 6th string/9th fret = C♯.

▶ *Flats are one fret lower:* 6th string/5th fret = A, so 6th string/4th fret = A♭; 6th string/10th fret = D, so 6th string/9th fret = D♭.

HOW?

▶ *Fretboard markings help.* Most guitars have fretboard inlays or marks somewhere on the neck indicating the 5th, 7th, 10th and 12th frets.

DO IT!

▶ *Start by memorizing the 6th and 5th strings.* You will need these notes very soon, for
ROADMAP #3.

SUMMING UP—NOW YOU KNOW...

▶ *The location of the notes on the fretboard.*

▶ *The meaning of these musical terms:*

whole step, half step, sharp, flat.

#2 THE MAJOR SCALE

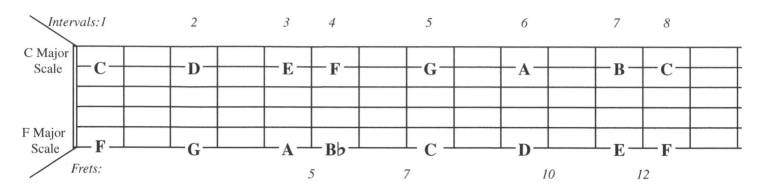

WHY?

▶ To understand music and to communicate with other players, you need to know about the major scale. The major scale is a ruler that helps you measure distances between notes and chords. Knowing the major scale will help you understand and talk about chord construction, scales and chord relationships.

WHAT?

▶ *The major scale is the "Do–Re–Mi" scale you have heard all your life.* Countless familiar tunes are composed of notes from this scale.

▶ *Intervals are distances between notes.* The intervals of the major scale are used to describe these distances. For example, E is the third note of the C major scale, and it is four frets above C (see above). This distance is called a *third*. Similarly, A is a third above F, and C♯ is a third above A. On the guitar, *a third is always a distance of four frets.*

HOW?

▶ *Every major scale has the same interval pattern of whole and half-steps:*

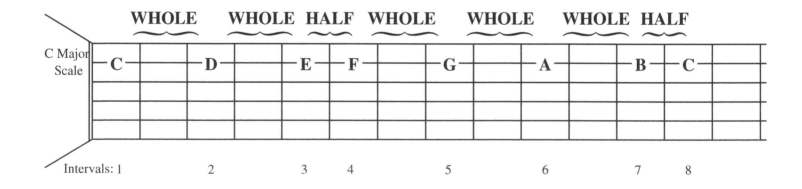

In other words, the major scale ascends by whole steps (two frets at a time) with two exceptions: there is a half step (one fret) from the third to the fourth notes and from the seventh to the eighth notes.

► *Every interval can be described in terms of frets.* For example, a major third is 4 frets. Some intervals, such as 9th, 11th and 13th, extend above the octave:

C Major Scale

Intervals:

1	2	3	4	5	6	7	8	9	10	11	12	13

| C | D | E | F | G | A | B | C | D | E | F | G | A |

Frets: 5   7   10   12   15   17   20

DO IT!

* ► *Play any note and find the note that is a third higher, a fourth and fifth higher,* etc. Do this by counting up the right amount of frets on a single string.

SUMMING UP — NOW YOU KNOW...

► *The intervals of the major scale.*

► *The number of frets that make up each interval.*

* The numbers in diamonds refer to tracks on the recording that accompanies this book.

TWO MOVEABLE MAJOR CHORDS

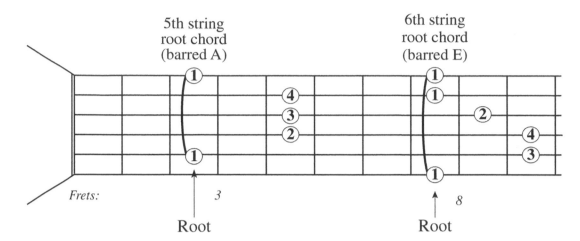

WHY?

▶ Moveable chords have no open (unfretted) strings, so they can be played (moved) all over the fretboard. The two moveable chords of **ROADMAP #3** will get you started playing chords up and down the neck.

WHAT?

▶ A *chord* is a group of three or more notes played simultaneously.

▶ A *moveable chord* can be played all over the fretboard. It contains no open (unfretted) strings.

▶ A *root* is the note that gives a chord its name. The root of all C chords (C7, C minor, C augmented, etc.) is C.

HOW?

▶ *The 6th string identifies the 6th-string root chord.* It's G when played at the 3rd fret, because the 6th string/3rd fret is G. At the 6th fret, it's B♭, and so on.

▶ *The 5th string identifies the 5th-string root chord.* It's C at the 3rd fret because the 5th string/3rd fret is C. At the 9th fret, it's F♯ (G♭), and so on.

DO IT!

▶ *Play the 6th-string root chords all over the fretboard,* naming the chords as you play them.

▶ *Play the 5th-string root chords all over the fretboard* and name them.

▶ *Play this 12-bar blues progression using 6th-string root chords.* It fits thousands of blues and R&B tunes, including "Everyday, I Have the Blues," "Kansas City," "Shake, Rattle and Roll," "Johnny B. Goode" and "Dust My Broom." Hum one of these tunes while you strum once for each slash:

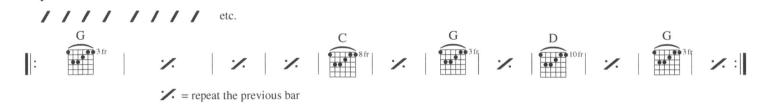

✗. = repeat the previous bar

4 ▶ *Play the same basic blues progression using 5th string root chords.*

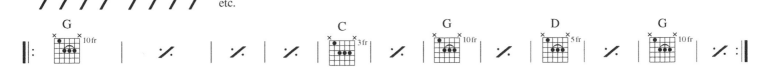

▶ *Play it in different keys.* This is easy if you observe the fret distances (intervals) between chords. For example, the second chord (C) in the twelve-bar blues progression is five frets above (or seven frets below) the first chord (G). This is true in all keys. The other chord in the progression is two frets above the second chord. This is also true in any key.

Key of F:

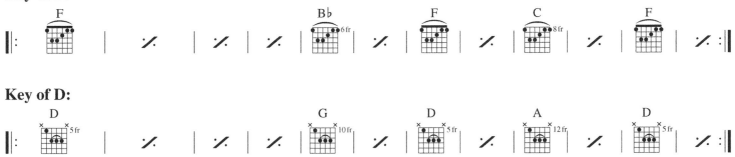

Key of D:

▶ *Play this 8 bar progression in several keys.* It matches "How Long Blues," "Sittin' on Top of the World," "It Hurts Me Too," "Come Back Baby," "You Gotta Move," "Keys to the Highway," and "Come on in My Kitchen."

Key of C:

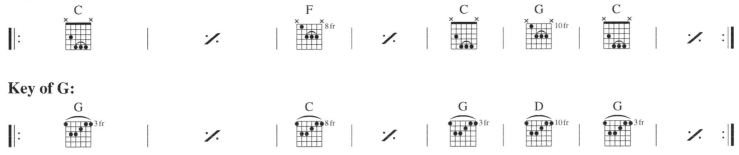

Key of G:

SUMMING UP—NOW YOU KNOW...

▶ *The intervals that make up a major chord* (the 1st, 3rd and 5th).

▶ *How to play any major chord two ways:* Using a moveable chord with a 6th string root and a moveable chord with a 5th string root.

▶ *How to play basic 12- and 8-bar blues progressions in any key.*

▶ *The meaning of these musical terms:*

chord, moveable chord, root.

VARIATIONS OF THE TWO MOVEABLE MAJOR CHORDS

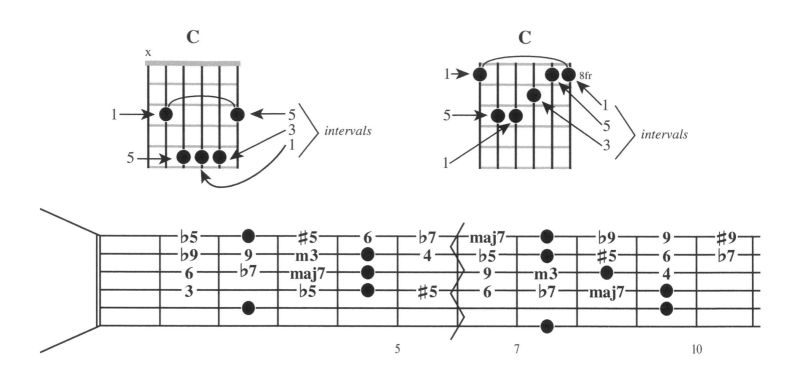

WHY

▶ You can play dozens of hip blues chords (ninths, minor sevenths, etc.) by altering slightly the two basic moveable major chords of **ROADMAP #3** (e.g., lower one string one fret to flat a third—this changes the major chord to a minor chord). This is an easy way to expand your chord vocabulary.

WHAT?

▶ *The two moveable major chords (and all major chords) consist of roots, 3rds and 5ths.* Make sure you know the intervals in these two formations. The chord grids above **ROADMAP #4** identify the intervals (e.g., the 5th and 2nd strings in the barred E formation are 5ths).

▶ *You can relate other intervals (4ths, 7ths, etc.) to the intervals you already know:* A 4th is one fret higher than a 3rd, and a 6th is two frets higher than a 5th.

HOW?

▶ *Compare every new chord you learn to a basic chord you already know.* Every small chord grid in the "DO IT" section, below, is a variation of a basic chord formation.

DO IT!

▶ *Here are the most-played blues chord grids.* Play them and compare each formation to the larger grid to the left, from which it is derived.

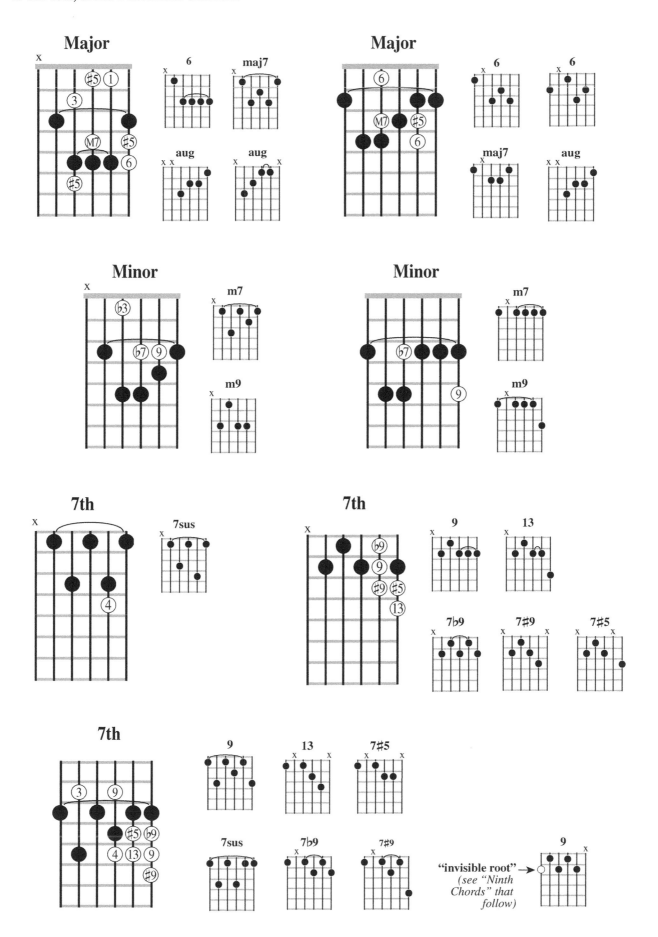

▶ *Ninth chords* are an important element in urban, electric blues guitar. Backup guitarists play two "sliding licks"* that are based on ninth chords.

▷ In one lick you play a 5th string root/ninth chord and slide the top three strings up and down two frets:

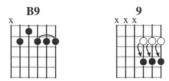

▷ In the other lick, you play the 6th string root ninth chord and slide the 4th, 3rd and 2nd strings up and down two frets. This chord form doesn't include a root note, but you can locate it by visualizing the absent 6th string root:

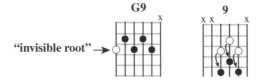

▷ Here's a typical backup part that uses these sliding licks:

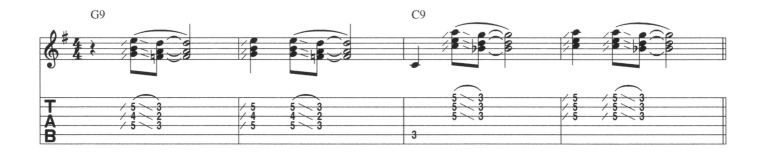

SUMMING UP—NOW YOU KNOW...

▶ *Two ways to play several chord types—with a 5th string root and a 6th string root.*

▶ *Two popular sliding ninth chord licks.*

A lick is a brief musical phrase.

#5 THE I–IV–V CHORD FAMILY

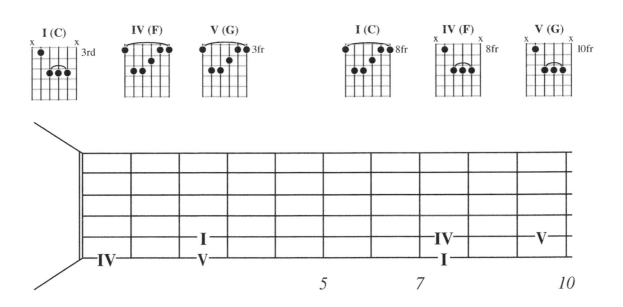

WHY?

▶ The **I–IV–V chord family** is the basis for countless blues chord progressions. This chart shows you how to locate chord families automatically in any key, all over the fretboard.

WHAT?

▶ *The Roman numerals in the chart above are the roots of the I, IV and V chords in the key of C.*

▶ *The numbers I, IV and V refer to the major scale of your key.*

HOW?

▶ *The I–IV–V root patterns in the fretboard chart are moveable.*

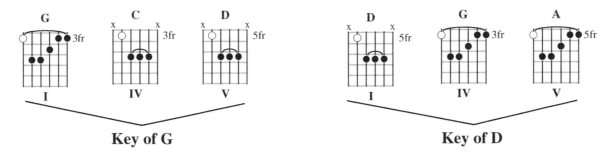

▶ *Variations of the two moveable major chords can be used in the chord family.* Blues tunes often consist of seventh or ninth chords, instead of major chords. There are also minor key blues songs in which the I and IV chords, or all three chords, are minors or minor 7ths. *Regardless of these variations, the I–IV–V root relationships are the same.* Here are some sample chord families. They are all in the key of G and all roots are white circles.

(Sample chord families in key of G)

DO IT!

▶ *Play several chord families two ways:* First with a 6th string root/I chord, then with a 5th string root/I chord. For example, the four chord families shown earlier have 6th string root/I chords. Here are the same chord families with 5th string root/I chords:

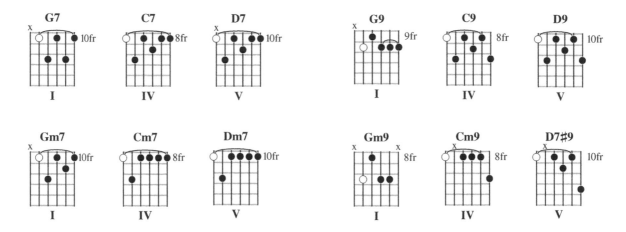

▶ *Play the 12-bar blues progression in several keys.* This very important progression, mentioned in **ROADMAP #3,** can be understood in terms of the I–IV–V chord family:

▷ There are three 4-bar phrases in the blues progession.

▷ The first phrase is 4 bars of the I chord.

▷ The second phrase starts with 2 bars of the IV chord and ends with 2 bars of the I chord. Often, the lyrics of the first phrase are repeated.

▷ The third phrase starts with 2 bars of the V chord and ends with 2 bars of the I chord. The lyrics of the third phrase usually rhyme with (and complete the thought of) the first two phrases.

Play this pattern in several keys. The sample below is in E♭.

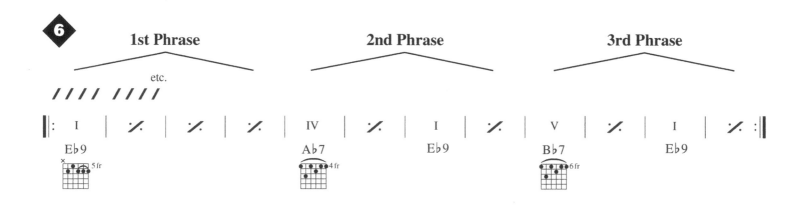

► *Variations of the 12-bar blues*

▷ In many 12-bar blues, bar 2 of the first phrase is the IV chord.

▷ Often, the second bar of the third phrase is the IV chord.

▷ The last two bars of the third phrase usually consist of an ending phrase called a *turnaround,* which ends with a V chord. The turnaround sets up the next verse, which repeats the 12-bar format.

► *Play the 12-bar blues in many keys using these variations,* like this sample in A:

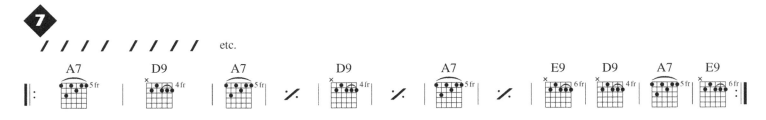

► *Play the 8-bar blues in several keys.* Here's the typical 8-bar pattern:

► *Boogie woogie lick:* This backup lick that is so fundamental to blues and rock is based on the two moveable chords of **ROADMAP #3** and the chord families of this chapter. The barred chords are abbreviated to two-note formations, and the little finger of your fretting hand adds extra, alternating (on-and-off) notes:

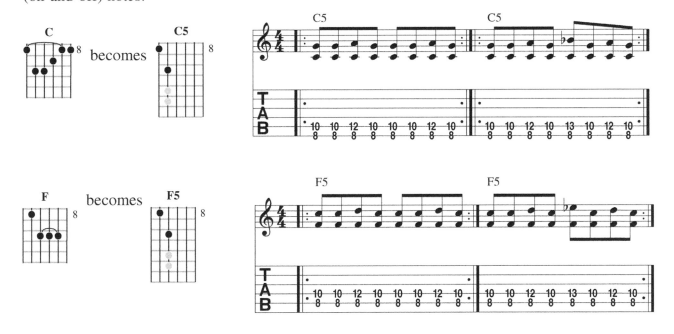

► The abbreviated chords with a "5" in their names (C5, F5) consist of a root and fifth, but no third. This makes them different from most major chords.

♪ *Use the boogie woogie lick as a backup for blues tunes.* Hum "How Long Blues," "Sittin' on Top of the World" and other 8-bar blues tunes mentioned previously, while playing the boogie licks below. Then do it in different keys, with a 6th string root/I chord and with a 5th string root/I chord.

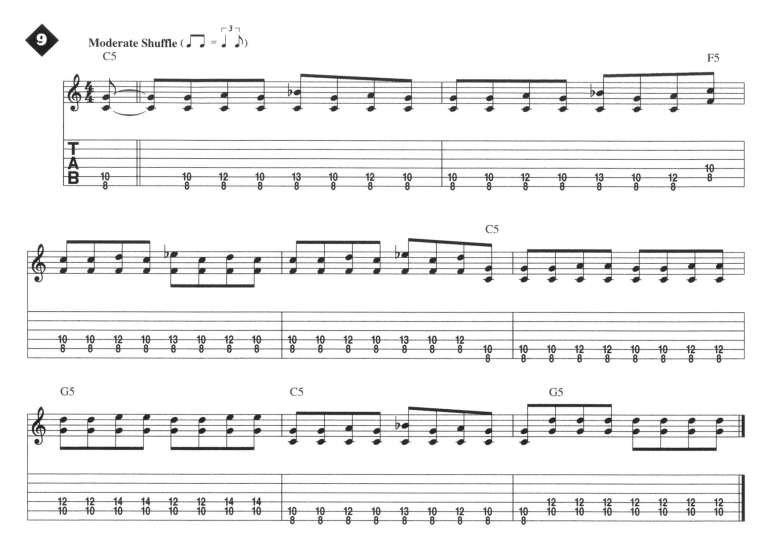

SUMMING UP—NOW YOU KNOW...

► *Two different ways to play the I–IV–V chord family in any key* with a 6th string root/I chord and a 5th string root/I chord.

► *How to play the 12-bar and 8-bar blues progressions in any key, two ways.*

► *How to use many bluesy chord variations within the I–IV–V chord families.*

► *How to play the boogie woogie lick in any key.*

► *The meaning of these musical terms:*

I chord, IV chord, V chord, chord family, 12-bar blues, 8-bar blues, boogie woogie backup.

◆#6 THE F–D–A ROADMAP

All F Chords:

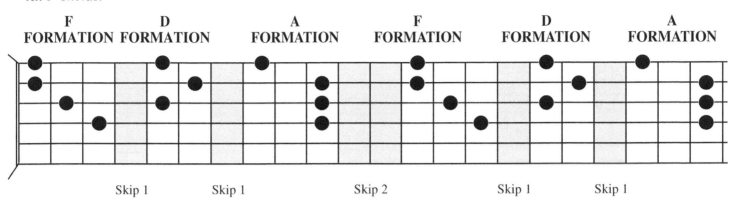

F FORMATION	D FORMATION	A FORMATION	F FORMATION	D FORMATION	A FORMATION

Skip 1   Skip 1   Skip 2   Skip 1   Skip 1

WHY?

▶ ***The F–D–A Roadmap shows you how to play any major chord all over the fretboard,*** using three major chord formations. It enables you to automatically "climb the fretboard," playing rapidly ascending or descending licks.

WHAT?

▶ The chords in the fretboard diagram above are all F chords.

HOW?

▶ ***To memorize this roadmap, remember: F–SKIP 1, D–SKIP 1, A–SKIP 2.*** In other words, play an F formation, skip one fret, play a D formation, skip one fret, play an A formation, skip two frets.

Use the F–D–A Roadmap to play all the D chords:

All D Chords:

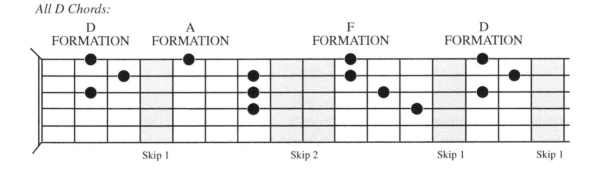

D FORMATION	A FORMATION	F FORMATION	D FORMATION

Skip 1   Skip 2   Skip 1   Skip 1

▶ Notice that you can climb the fretboard *starting with any chord formation.* The F–D–A Roadmap is a continuous loop that you can enter at any point. It can be the D–A–F or A–F–D Roadmap. The "skips" are always the same: one skip after F, one after D, two after A.

► *You can make the three shapes into sevenths.* This is how they are often played in the blues:

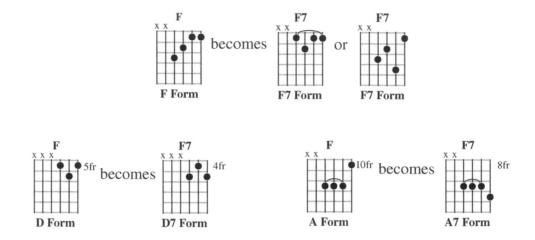

DO IT!

► The following blues licks make use of the F–D–A Roadmap:

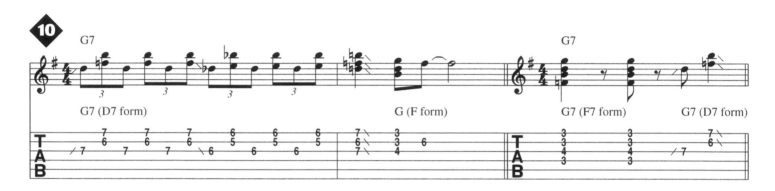

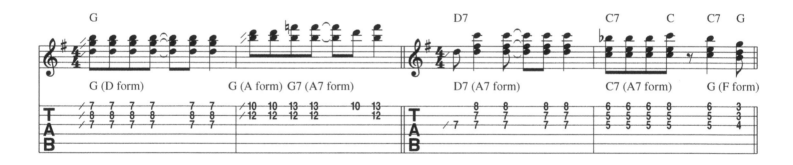

► Fingerpicking blues guitarists love the keys of E, A and D, because they can add open E, A and D bass notes (on the three lowest strings) to chord fragments that are played on the three highest strings. Here are some sample licks:

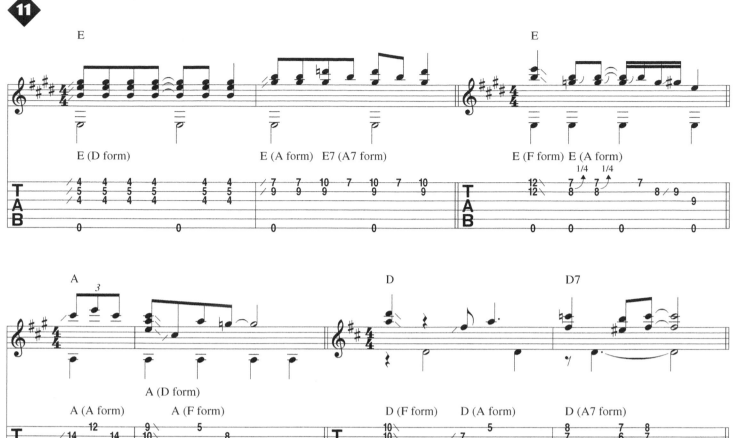

SUMMING UP–NOW YOU KNOW...

▶ *How to play three major chord fragments.*

▶ *How to use them to play any major chord all over the fretboard* (with the F–D–A Roadmap).

▶ *How to alter the major chord fragments to play 7th chords.*

▶ *How to play moveable blues licks using chord fragments.*

#7 FIRST POSITION BLUES BOXES

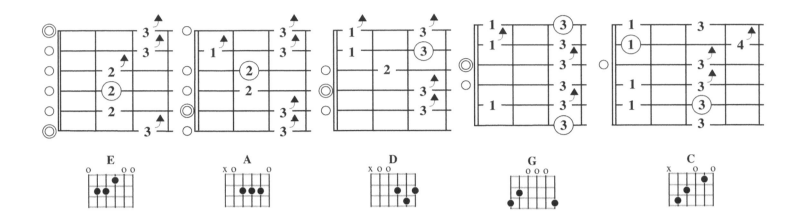

WHY?

▶ Each key has its own blues scale, which is used for playing melodies and licks. To play blues in first position, you need to know the five scales above. Acoustic blues players have always based their playing on these scales, and the great rock and electric blues guitarists also use them.

WHAT?

▶ *Every key has its own scale and characteristic licks.* You only use the C scale to play in the key of C, the E scale to play in E, and so on.

▶ *Each scale (and the licks that go with it) can be played throughout a tune,* in spite of chord changes within the tune.

▶ *The root notes in each scale are circled.* The numbers are suggested fingerings.

▶ *The scale notes with bends (2ᐃ, 3ᐃ) can be stretched or choked.* This left-hand technique, in which you pull a string up or down with your fretting finger to raise its pitch, is a very important blues sound.

▶ *The above scales are pentatonic,* which means each scale contains five notes: the 1st (root), ♭3rd, 4th, 5th and ♭7th notes of your key. The notes in the C pentatonic blues scale are: C (1st or root), E♭ (♭3rd), F (4th), G (5th), and B♭ (♭7th).

▶ ***However, you can add other notes and still sound bluesy.*** Each blues scale is a starting point. You'll find expanded versions of each scale, with "extra notes" added, in the "HOW" section that follows.

HOW?

▶ ***Put your hand "in position" for each scale by fingering the appropriate chord*** (e.g., play an E chord to get in position for the E blues scale). You don't have to maintain the chord while playing the scale, but it's a reference point.

▶ ***Play "up and down" each scale (as written below) until it feels comfortable and familiar.*** Here are the five scales to practice:

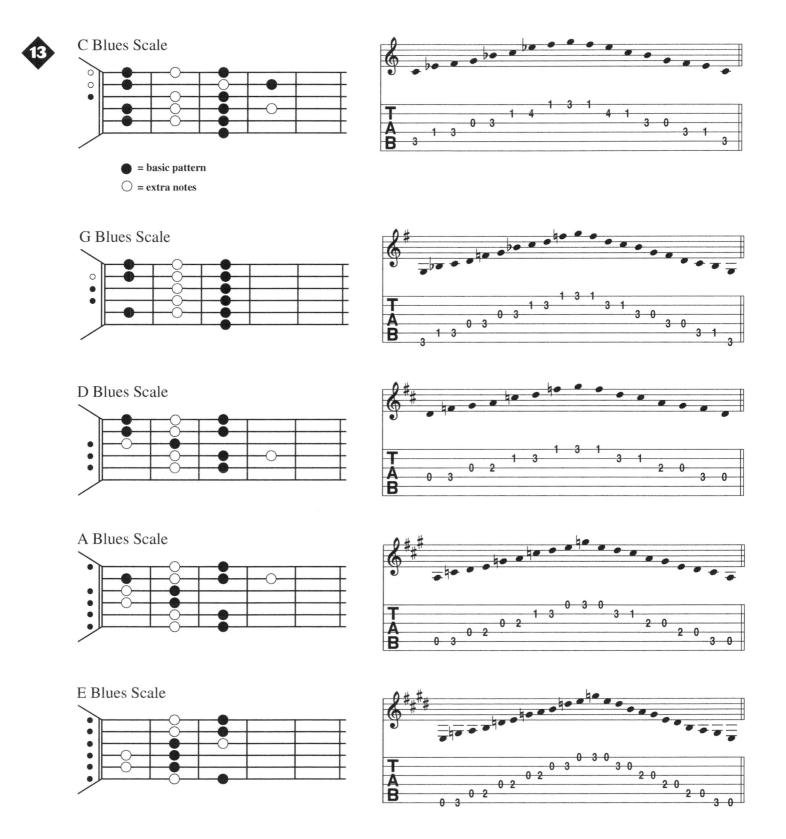

C Blues Scale

● = basic pattern
○ = extra notes

G Blues Scale

D Blues Scale

A Blues Scale

E Blues Scale

DO IT!

▶ The following solos show how to use all five blues scales to play some classic licks. All five make use of the 8-bar blues format described in **ROADMAP #3** and **ROADMAP #5**. In true country blues fashion, they involve some fingerpicking:

▷ *The thumb thumps out bass notes,* playing a low root note on most of the downbeats (there are four per bar.) This is basic "Texas style" fingerpicking.

▷ *The fingers play licks on the treble strings.* Some pickers use the index finger, others play the 1st string with the middle finger and the 2nd, 3rd and 4th strings with the index.

▷ *Most of the licks come from the first position major scale of your I chord,* but you finger the chords that are indicated as well (I, IV and V). In this style of blues picking, you play lead, rhythm and bass all at once!

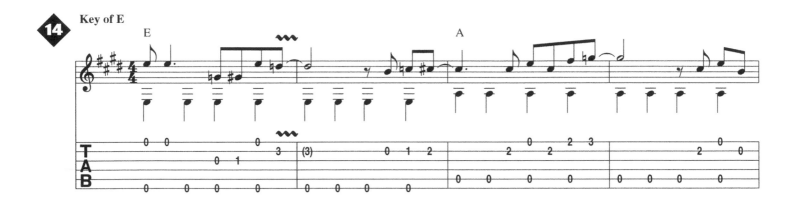

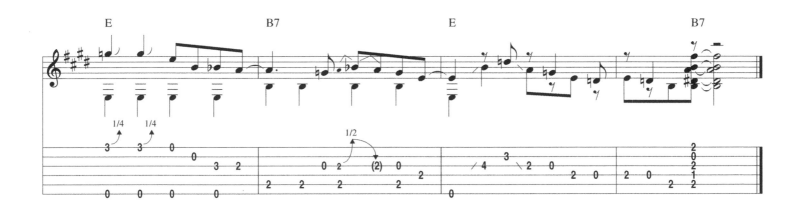

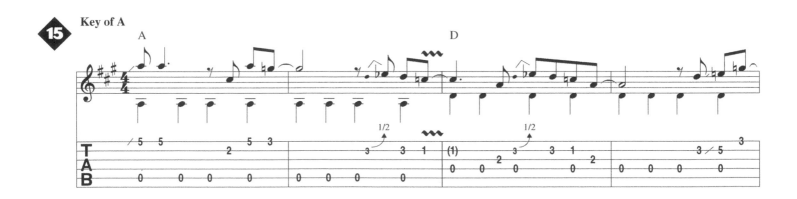

22

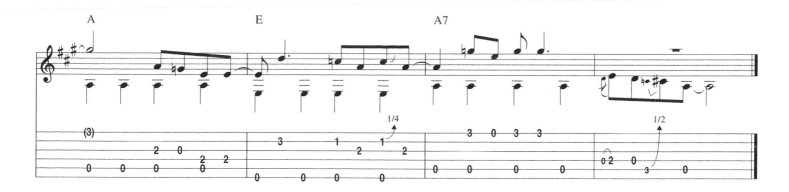

Key of D

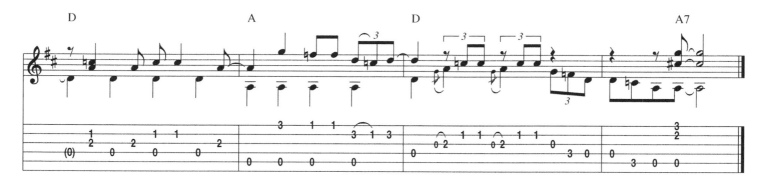

Key of G

▶ *Play along with the first two Practice Tracks,* which are in the keys of E and A. Listen to the lead guitar for licks and ideas, then tune it out on your stereo and play similar licks with just the backup band track.

SUMMING IT UP—NOW YOU KNOW…

▶ *How to stretch strings for a bluesy effect.*

▶ *The notes that make up the pentatonic blues scale.*

▶ *How to play blues licks and scales in five different keys.*

▶ *How to play basic "Texas style" blues fingerpicking.*

THE FIRST AND SECOND MOVEABLE BLUES BOXES

#8

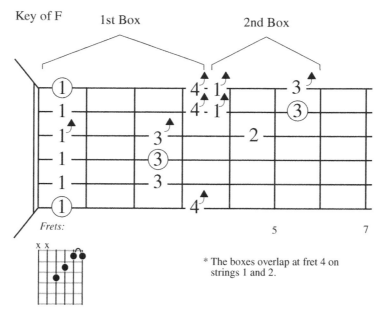

Key of F   1st Box   2nd Box

* The boxes overlap at fret 4 on strings 1 and 2.

WHY?

▶ Like the first position blues scales of **ROADMAP #7**, these scales, often called *blues boxes,* are the basis for blues licks, solos and melodies. Since they include no unfretted strings, you can move them around the fretboard and use them to play in all keys. Countless well-known blues and rock riffs and solos are based on the first and second blues boxes. They are at the heart of modern electric blues guitar and are useful for acoustic players.

WHAT?

▶ *The two blues boxes above are F blues scales.* The root notes are circled. The numbers indicate suggested fingering positions.

▶ *The scale notes with bends* $(4^{\uparrow}, 1^{\uparrow})$ *can be stretched or choked.* (See **ROADMAP #7**).

▶ Like the first-position blues scales, *the blues boxes are useful for jamming and for playing melodies and licks.* You can solo in one blues box throughout a blues song (and many a non-blues song), in spite of chord changes.

▶ Like the first-position blues scales, *the blues boxes are pentatonic,* but you can add other notes and still sound bluesy. Here's an expanded version of the two boxes with "extra notes":

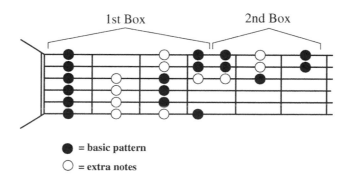

1st Box   2nd Box

● = basic pattern

○ = extra notes

25

► ***The first blues box is a moveable version of the first position E blues scale.*** Note the similarity:

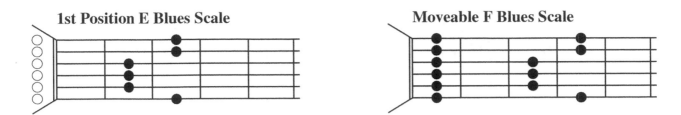

1st Position E Blues Scale   **Moveable F Blues Scale**

► ***The second blues box allows you to play in a higher register than the first box.*** It has the same five notes as the first box, but it's further up the fretboard. Also, like every blues box, it lends itself to certain licks and has a flavor of its own.

HOW?

► ***To put your left hand in position for the first blues box, play an F formation at the appropriate fret:*** To get in position for a G blues scale, play an F-formation/G chord (at the third fret). You don't have to maintain the F chord position while playing the scale, but it's a helpful reference point and it contains a high and low root note.

First Blues Box—Key of G

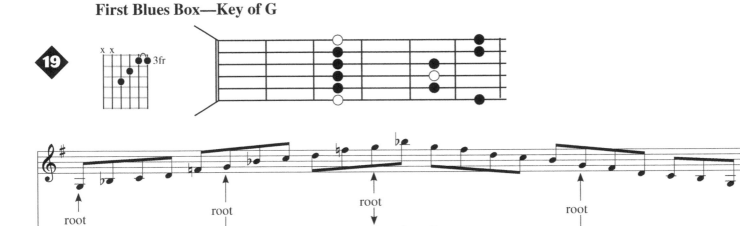

► ***Here are some typical first blues box licks in G:***

26

▶ ***Double-stops add depth and flavor to first blues box licks.*** T-Bone Walker played double-note licks in the '40s and Chuck Berry popularized them in the '50s. Play the altered, double-note G blues box and licks below:

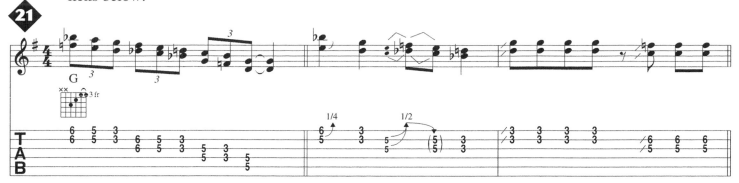

▶ ***Here's an 8-bar blues shuffle in B♭ that relies heavily on double-note licks:***

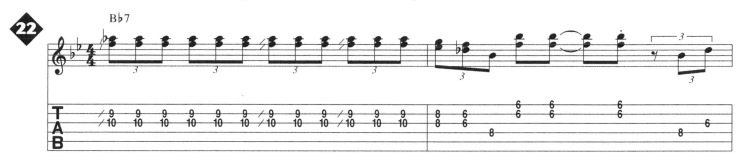

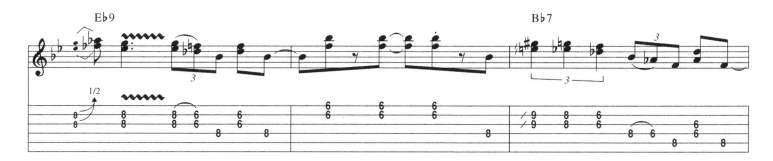

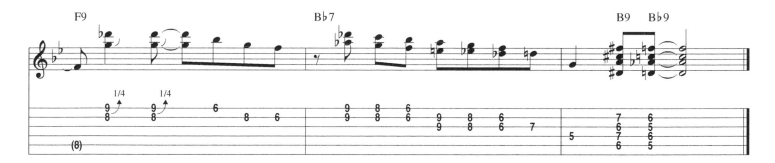

▶ ***To put your left hand in position for the second blues box, play the root note on the second string with your third (ring) finger.*** In G, play the G note on the 2nd string/8th fret with your ring finger.

Second Blues Box—Key of G

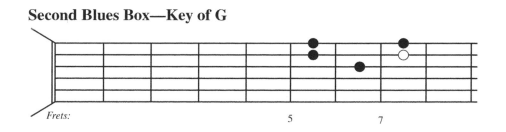

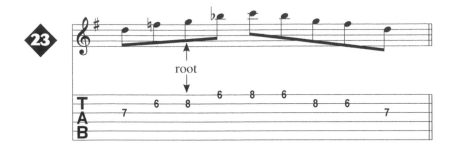

▶ *You can use the chord fragments of* **ROADMAP #6** *to go from the first blues box to the second.* For instance, to be in position for the first box, in the key of G, play the F formation/G chord. Then, for the second box, move up to the D7 formation/G7 chord.

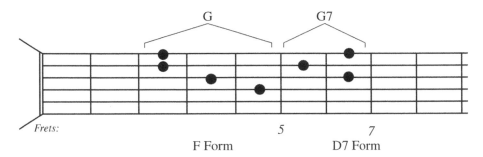

▶ *The second box lends itself to Albert King-type licks.* Here are some typical second blues box licks in G:

Back and forth between the 1st and 2nd box

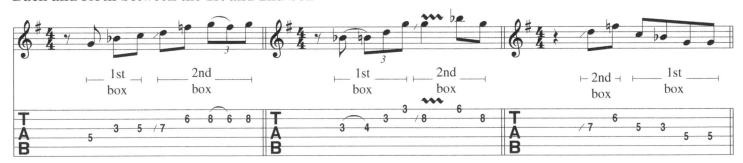

DO IT!

▶ *Experiment with the licks and scales of these two blues boxes* and play along with your favorite blues recordings. Figure out a song's key and use the appropriate box. A hint about finding a song's key— listen for the chord that "resolves" the tune, i.e., the ending chord. If the song fades out, find the chord on which the song *could* end.

▶ *Play along with the Practice Tracks, using the two blues boxes.*

► *Learn the following solo,* which illustrates the use of the first two blues boxes in a typical 12-bar blues. It's in the key of A.

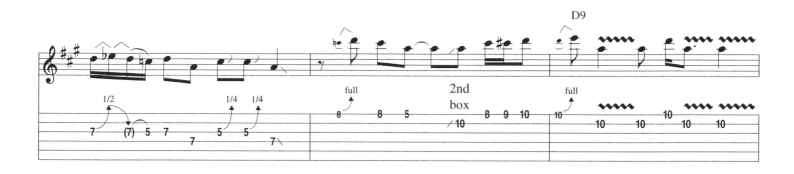

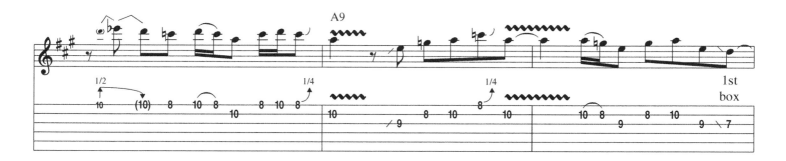

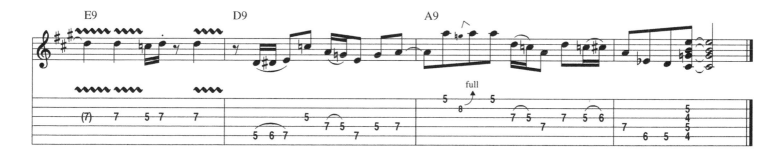

SUMMING UP—NOW YOU KNOW...

► *Two moveable blues boxes.*

► *A lot of licks that go with each box.*

► *How to use the boxes to improvise single-note solos in any key.*

9

THE THIRD AND FOURTH MOVEABLE BLUES BOXES

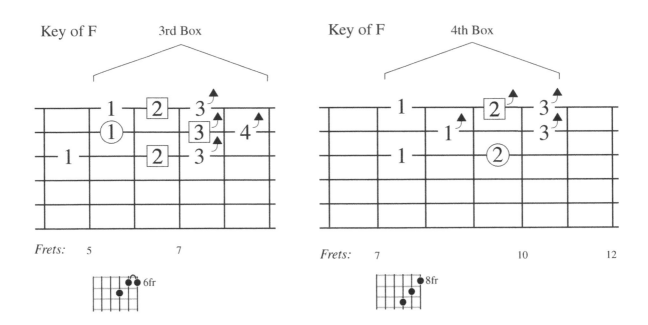

WHY?

▶ Like the blues boxes of **ROADMAP #8,** these two moveable scale positions help you play blues licks and solos all over the fretboard. Once you're familiar with them, you can play in four positions in any key, getting higher up the neck as you progress from the first to the fourth position.

WHAT?

▶ *The two blues boxes above are F blues scales.* As in **ROADMAP #8,** the root notes are circled. The numbers indicate suggested fingering positions.

▶ *The scale notes with bends* (4↑ʌ1↑) *be stretched or choked.*

▶ *"Extra notes," written in squares,* are not in the pentatonic blues scale, but they are often played in these scale positions.

▶ *You can solo with either of these boxes throughout a blues song* (and many a non-blues song), in spite of chord changes—just like the first two boxes.

▶ *The third blues box lends itself to B.B. King-type licks.* It has a more *major* sound than the other boxes. In fact, it can be useful in rock or country tunes, even when the other blues boxes sound inappropriate, but it can also wail in a blues song.

▶ *The third and fourth blues boxes are in a higher register than the first two,* and each box has its own unique bends, hammer-ons and pull-offs.

HOW?

▶ *To put your left hand in position for the third blues box, play the F formation/IV chord of your key:*
In the key of G, play an F formation/C chord (at the 8th fret), because C is the IV chord of G. Or, play
the tonic (the key note, such as a G note in the key of G) on the 2nd string with your index finger.

Third Blues Box—Key of G

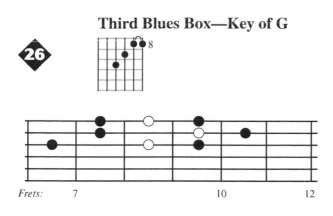

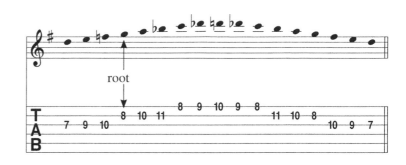

▶ *Here are some typical third blues box licks in G:*

▶ *To put your left hand in position for the fourth blues box, play the tonic on the third string with your
middle finger.* In G, play the G note on the 3rd string/12th fret with your middle finger.

Fourth Blues Box—Key of G

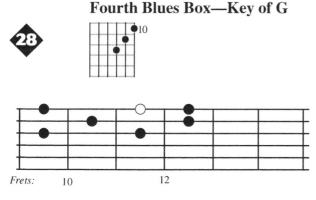

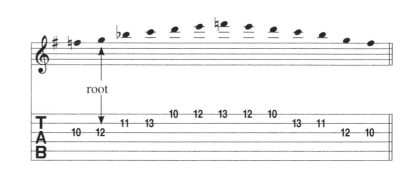

▶ *You can also relate the fourth position to this minor chord fragment,* which is an abbreviated version
of the 5th string root/minor chord.

Minor Chord Fragment

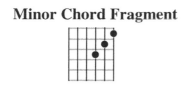

5th String Root/Minor Chord

To find the fourth position in the key of G, play the abbreviated 5th string root/Gm:

Gm

▶ *Here are some typical fourth blues box licks in the key of G:*

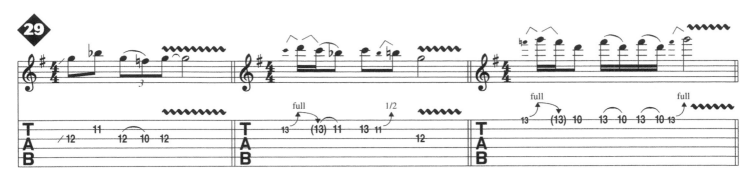

DO IT!

▶ *Experiment with the licks and scales of these two blues boxes* and play along with your favorite blues recordings.

▶ *Play along with the Practice Tracks, using the third and fourth blues boxes.*

▶ *Learn the following solo,* which illustrates the use of the third and fourth blues boxes in a jazzy 8-bar blues.

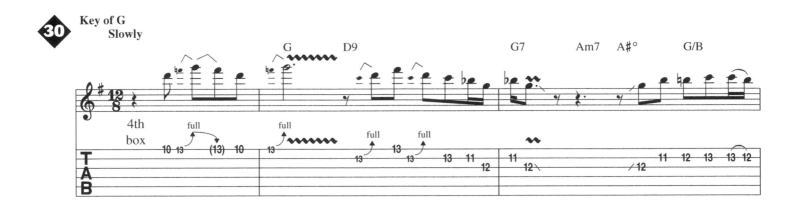

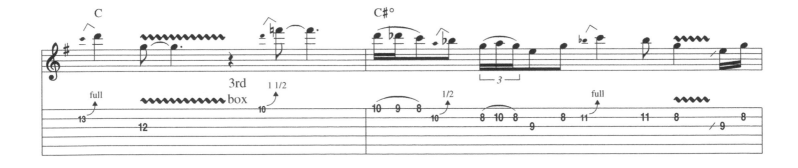

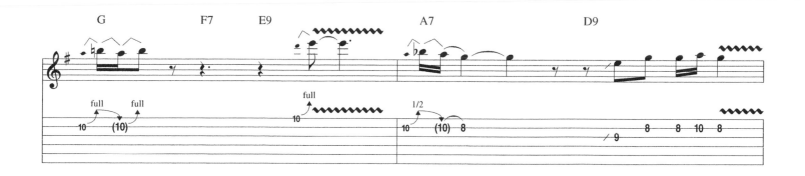

SUMMING UP—NOW YOU KNOW...

▶ *The meaning of the musical term "tonic."*

▶ *Two more moveable blues boxes.*

▶ *A lot of licks that go with each box.*

▶ *How to use four different blues positions to improvise single-note solos in any key.*

MOVEABLE TURNAROUNDS AND BACKUP LICKS

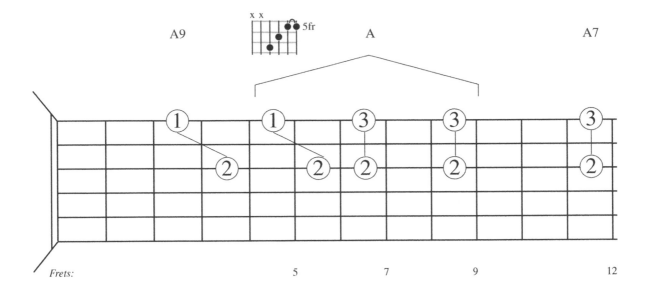

WHY?

▶ This moveable double-note pattern opens up a whole "bag of licks." It's the source of many classic blues riffs and turnarounds.

WHAT?

▶ *It's basically a key-of-E blues turnaround made into a moveable lick.* Here's the original turnaround, followed by the moveable version:

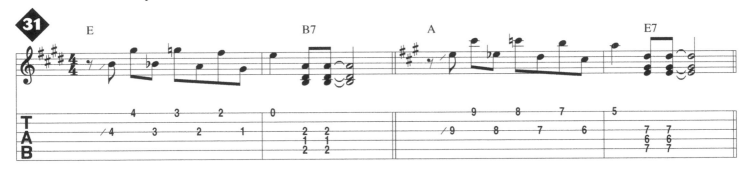

▶ *"Home base" for this series of licks is the F formation.*

▶ *There are countless variations of this turnaround lick*—it can go up or down, or up and down, as these variations on an A chord show:

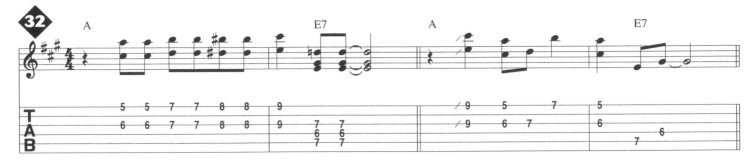

► *These licks can be played at any time in a tune,* not just at the turnaround. They are used as backup licks, as *riffs* (repetitious signature licks that give a tune a distinct character) and in solos.

HOW?

► *Change F formations with the tune's chord changes.* When there is a C chord, position your fretting hand at the 8th fret/F formation (C), and play double-note licks from this "home base."

► *You can start a lick at any of the five positions of* **ROADMAP #10,** not just at the F formation. You can also play double-notes "in-between" the indicated positions, as the examples that follow will show.

DO IT!

► *Here are some ways the double-note lick can be used.* Below there are two riffs and a 12 bar folk/blues tune with double-note fills played during pauses in the vocal line:

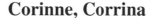

Corinne, Corrina

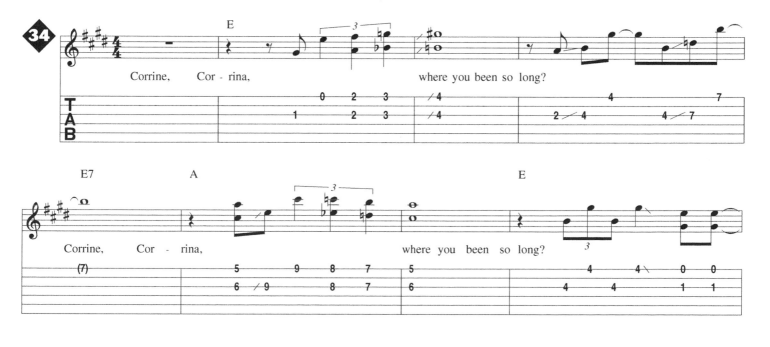

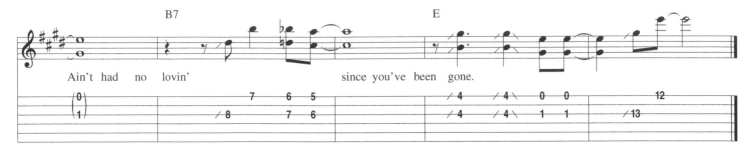

Ain't had no lovin'   since you've been gone.

▶ *Here are some useful first-position and moveable turnarounds:*

SUMMING UP—NOW YOU KNOW...

▶ *How to play a series of double-note licks on the 1st and 3rd strings for solos or backup, in any key.*

▶ *The meaning of the musical term "riff."*

▶ *Many first-position and moveable turnarounds.*

BOOGIE WOOGIE LICKS: THE MAJOR PENTATONIC SCALE

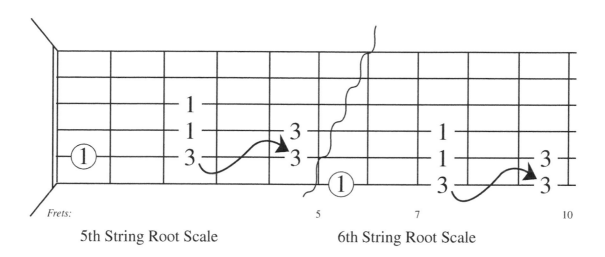

5th String Root Scale   6th String Root Scale

WHY?

▶   This scale, often used for soloing in rock and country music, is used in blues for boogie-woogie backup riffs.

WHAT?

▶   The two scales in **ROADMAP #11** are B♭ scales. *One has a 5th string root, the other has a 6th string root.* The root notes are circled.

▶   *The arrows indicate optional slides* from one note to another.

▶   *These pentatonic scales are major and contain no blue notes.** They consist of 1, 2, 3, 5 and 6. In the key of C that's: C(1), D(2), E(3), G(5) and A(6). Just hum the "My Girl" riff to remember the major pentatonic sound.

▶   *Blues players often add blue notes* to the major pentatonic scale, to create bluesy riffs. Here is **ROADMAP #11** with the blue notes added.

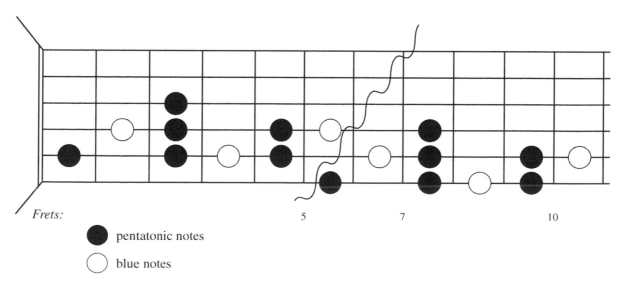

⬤ pentatonic notes

◯ blue notes

*Flatted thirds, flatted fifths and flatted sevenths often are called *blue notes.*

37

► *These scales are moveable versions of the first position E and A pentatonic scales* that acoustic blues guitarists use for boogie licks:

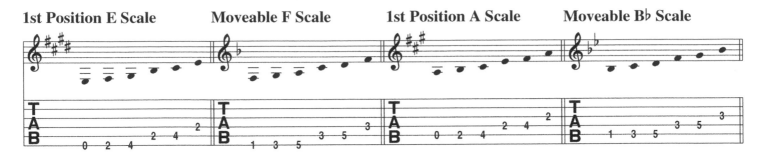

1st Position E Scale   **Moveable F Scale**   **1st Position A Scale**   **Moveable B♭ Scale**

HOW?

► *To create a blues riff, use a different scale for each chord.* A blues in the key of C has C(I), F(IV) and G(V) chords, so you'll use all three major pentatonic scales: C, F and G.

► *Play the same riff on each chord (the I, IV and V).* This gives the song a distinct sound.

► *Use the I-IV-V chord families of* **ROADMAP #5** *to locate your riffs.*

   ♪ Here's a typical boogie lick in the key of C, for all three chords. Since the I chord has a 6th string/8th fret root, the IV chord riff starts on the 5th string/8th fret. In other words, the IV chord riff is identical to the I chord but *"a string higher."* The V chord riff is the same as the IV chord riff, but *two frets higher.*

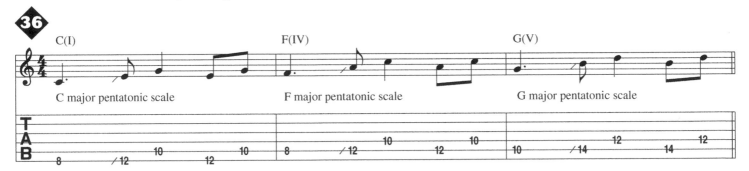

   ♪ If you start with a 5th string root/I chord, you get the following chord family of boogie riffs. The V chord riff is the same as the I chord riff, but *"a string lower."* The IV chord riff is the same as the V chord riff, but *two frets lower:*

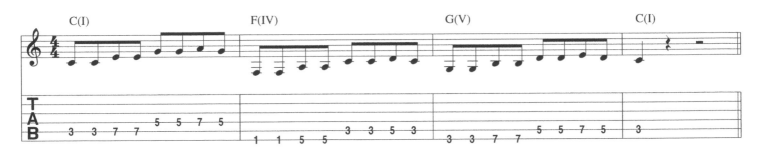

DO IT!

▶ *Play these boogie licks and transpose them to different keys.* They are all G riffs. Since they are moveable, you can easily find the related C and D riffs, or play them in any key.

▶ *Some boogie licks are based on the first blues box:*

SUMMING UP—NOW YOU KNOW...

▶ *Two moveable, major pentatonic scales: one with a 6th string root, the other with a 5th string root.*

▶ *How to use them to create many different boogie backup licks in any key.*

▶ *The meaning of the musical term "blue notes."*

♪ USING THE PRACTICE TRACKS

On the four practice tracks, the lead guitar is separated from the rest of the band—it's on one side of your stereo. You can tune it out and use the band as backup, trying out any soloing techniques you like. You can also imitate the lead guitar.

Here are the soloing ideas on each track:

 #1 *Acoustic 12-Bar Boogie in E* (1st position E licks)

 #2 *Slow, Acoustic 8-Bar Blues in A* (1st position A licks)

 #3 *12-Bar Blues/Rock in Am* (1st and 2nd blues box licks)

 #4 *Slow 8-Bar Blues in G* (3rd and 4th blues box licks)

 #5 *12-Bar Shuffle in C* (1st blues box/double note licks)